BUTTERFLY AND FRIENDS

AN ILLUSTRATED POEM

by

Tamara Martin

Illustrated by:
Sona & Jacob

FIRST EDITION

Little Red Acorns

Printed and bound in the USA

Layout and Cover Design: Michael Linnard, MCSD
Fonts used in this book: Times New Roman, Charlemagne Stad, Arial, Trajan Pro and Gill Sans MT.

First Edition, 2014, manufactured in USA
1 2 3 4 5 6 7 8 9 10 LSI 20 19 18 17 16 15 14

Illustrations: Sona & Jacob

A version of the poem "Butterfly and Friends" first appeared in Sundays in the South, *2006, by Tamara Martin and Vernice Quebodeaux, published by Little Red Tree Publishing.*

Previous books in this collection:

Book 1: The Little Turtle
Book 2: Little Robin Redbreast

Library of Congress Cataloging-in-Publication Data

Martin, Tamara, 1956-
  Butterfly and Friends / written by Tamara Martin, -- 1st ed.
    p. cm.
  ISBN 978-1-935656-32-6 (pbk. : alk. paper)
1. Butterfly--Juvenile poetry. 2. Children's poetry, American. II. Title.
  PS3613.A786235F54 2014
  811'.6--dc22
                    2014958952

Little Red Acorns

An imprint of

Little Red Tree Publishing, LLC
635 Ocean Avenue, New London, CT 06320
website: www.littleredtree.com

For my husband, Michael

For my children, Aimee and Eric

For my granddaughter, Eloise Jolie.

Tamara

Butterfly posed on bended knee

While friends looked on,

Ant and Flea.

"What's wrong, dear butterfly?"

They both asked in despair.

"I've lost my will to live,"

Butterfly said.

"I've completely lost my flair."

"What do you mean?"

Asked Flea, with concern.

"My best friends have left me."

Answered Butterfly, with discern.

"They're just on different paths—

They'll be gone a short while."

Butterfly was relieved

By Ant and Flea's explanation.

He fluttered his wings

With great exaltation.

The moral of this short reprise

Is to understand that

Life is a great surprise.

Wish friends well when

they do go.

They'll be back someday

to continue the show.

BUTTERFLY AND FRIENDS

Butterfly posed on bended knee
While friends looked on, Ant and Flea.

"What's wrong, dear friend?"
They both asked, in despair.

"I've lost my will to live,"
Butterfly said, "I've lost my flair."

"What do you mean?"
Asked Flea with concern.

"My best friends have left me."
Answered Butterfly with discern.

"They're just on different paths–
They'll be gone a short while."

Butterfly was relieved
By his friend's explanation.

He fluttered his wings
With great exaltation.

The moral of this short reprise
Is to understand that
Life is a great surprise.

Wish friends well when they do go.
They'll be back someday
to continue the show.

www.ingramcontent.com/pod-product-compliance
Lightning Source LLC
Chambersburg PA
CBHW040812300326

41914CB00065B/1527

* 9 7 8 1 9 3 5 6 5 6 3 2 6 *